MILITARY MACHINES

MILITARY AIRPLANES

by Melissa Abramovitz

Consulting Editor: Gail Saunders-Smith, PhD

Consultant: Raymond L. Puffer, PhD
Historian, Ret.
Edwards Air Force Base History Office

CAPSTONE PRESS
a capstone imprint

Pebble Plus is published by Capstone Press,
1710 Roe Crest Drive, North Mankato, Minnesota 56003.
www.capstonepub.com

Library of Congress Cataloging-in-Publication Data
Abramovitz, Melissa, 1954–
    Military airplanes / by Melissa Abramovitz.
        p. cm.—(Pebble plus. Military machines)
    Includes bibliographical references and index.
    Summary: "Simple text and full-color photographs describe various military airplanes"—Provided by publisher.
    ISBN 978-1-4296-7571-0 (library binding)
    ISBN 978-1-4296-7881-0 (paperback)
    1. Airplanes, Military—United States—Juvenile literature. I. Title.
    UG1243.A27 2012
    623.74'6097—dc23   2011021654

Editorial Credits
Erika L. Shores, editor; Kyle Grenz, designer; Kathy McColley, production specialist

Photo Credits
Corbis/George Hall, 13
U.S. Air Force photo by Airman Perry Aston, 7, Master Sgt. Kevin J. Gruenwald, 5, 19, Master Sgt. Linda C. Miller, 17,
    Staff Sgt. Tony R. Tolley, 11, Staff Sgt. Jacob N. Bailey, 15, Staff Sgt. Andy M. Kin, cover
U.S. Navy Photo by MC2 John P. Curtis, 21, MC3 Joe Painter, 9

Artistic Effects
Shutterstock: Hitdelight

Note to Parents and Teachers

The Military Machines series supports national science standards related to science, technology,
and society. This book describes and illustrates military airplanes. The images support early readers
in understanding the text. The repetition of words and phrases helps early readers learn new
words. This book also introduces early readers to subject-specific vocabulary words, which are
defined in the Glossary section. Early readers may need assistance to read some words and to use
the Table of Contents, Glossary, Read More, Internet Sites, and Index sections of the book.

Printed in the United States of America in North Mankato, Minnesota.

012013   007134R

Table of Contents

What Are Military Airplanes?

The U.S. Armed Forces uses airplanes to fight battles from the air. Military airplanes fly farther, faster, and higher than regular airplanes.

Parts of Military Airplanes

Wings lift airplanes upward.

Jet or propeller engines

on the wings push planes

forward through the air.

engine

engines

The tail steers and keeps

planes upright.

A tailhook stops F/A-18

Hornets when they land

on aircraft carrier ships.

tailhook

Planes take off and land

on heavy-duty wheels.

F-15 Eagles have three wheels.

C-5 Galaxies have 28 wheels.

F-15 Eagle

Airplanes in the Military

Fighter planes drop bombs and shoot missiles.

F/A-18 Hornet fighters drop bombs on land and sea targets.

F-22 fighter jets fight

and escape from battles.

These jets travel faster

than the speed of sound.

C-5 Galaxy cargo planes

take troops and supplies

wherever they're needed.

Galaxies can carry six helicopters

and 270 soldiers.

E-3 Sentry spy planes track enemy planes, ships, and ground forces. A Sentry's radar dome can find objects 250 miles (402 kilometers) away.

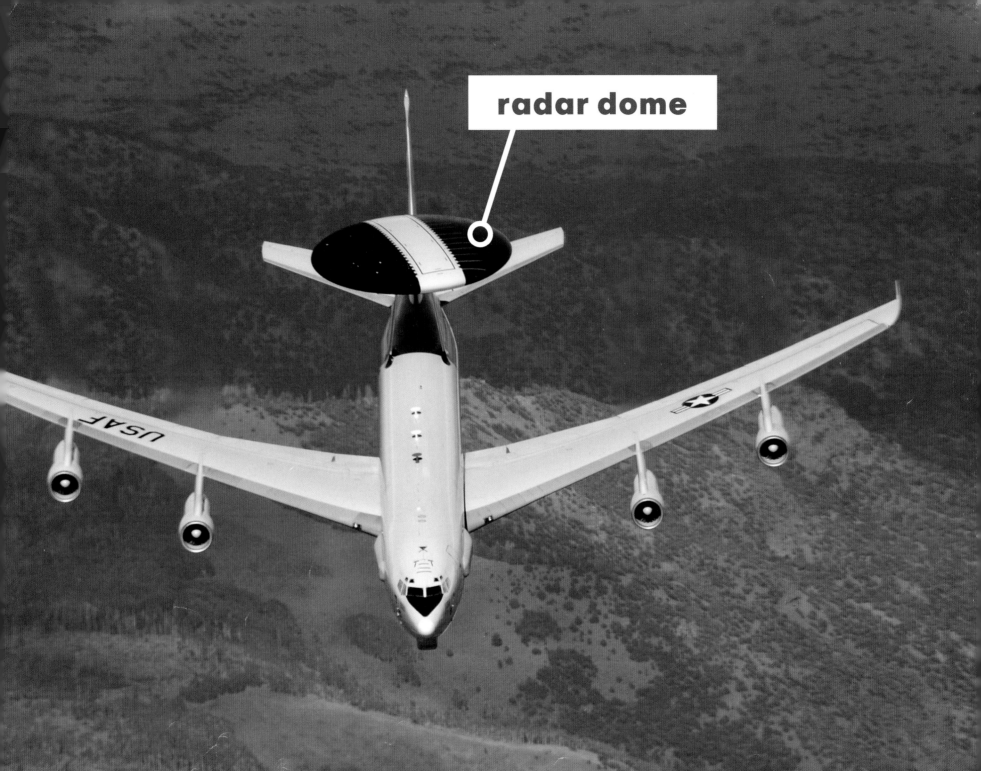

radar dome

Military Machines

Military airplanes work day
and night, over land and sea.
From speedy jets to giant cargo
carriers, military airplanes
are mighty machines.

Glossary

Armed Forces—the whole military; the U.S. Armed Forces include the Army, Navy, Air Force, Marine Corps, and Coast Guard

cargo—the goods carried by a vehicle

dome—a roof shaped like half of a ball

missile—a weapon that is fired at or dropped on a target

propeller—a set of rotating blades that provide the force to move an aircraft through the air

radar—a device that uses radio waves to track the location of objects

spy—to find out about enemies in a secret way

tailhook—a hook under a plane's tail that catches a cable wire to stop the plane when it lands on an aircraft carrier

Read More

Doman, Mary Kate. *Big Military Machines.* All about Big Machines. Berkeley Heights, N.J.: Enslow Publishers, 2012.

Simons, Lisa M. Bolt. *Airmen of the U.S. Air Force.* People of the U.S. Armed Forces. Mankato, Minn.: Capstone Press, 2009.

Zobel, Derek. *A-10 Thunderbolts.* Military Machines. Minneapolis: Bellwether Media, 2009.

Internet Sites

FactHound offers a safe, fun way to find Internet sites related to this book. All of the sites on FactHound have been researched by our staff.

Here's all you do:

Visit *www.facthound.com*

Type in this code: 9781429675710

Check out projects, games and lots more at **www.capstonekids.com**

Index

Word Count: 174

Grade: 1

Early-Intervention Level: 20